The Downstairs Dance Floor

The Downstairs Dance Floor

Taylor Graham

Texas Review Press
Huntsville, Texas

FIRST EDITION, 2006

Requests for permission to reproduce material from this work should be
sent to:

Permissions
Texas Review Press
English Department
Sam Houston State University
Huntsville, TX 77341-2146

Acknowledgments:

These poems—some in earlier versions—first appeared or are forthcoming in the
following publications:

Free Lunch
Fulva Flava
The Horsethief's Journal
International Poetry Review
Iron Horse Literary Review
Louisiana Literature
Newsletter Inago
Painted Hills Review
Paterson Literary Review
The Persistent Mirage
Poetry Depth Quarterly
Poetry Magazine
Vernacular

Cover design by Paul Ruffin

Library of Congress Cataloging-in-Publication Data

Graham, Taylor.
  The downstairs dance floor / Taylor Graham. -- 1st ed.
     p. cm.
  ISBN-13: 978-1-881515-94-4 (pbk. : alk. paper)
  ISBN-10: 1-881515-94-X (pbk. : alk. paper)
  I. Title.
  PS3557.R2228D69 2006
  371.9'04334--dc22
                              2006013093

In memory of my parents, Peg & Kenneth M. Taylor,

and for Hatch, my dance partner

Table of Contents

The Downstairs Dance Floor

The Dead Dancing

In her Spanish shawl, my mother swirls
in Heber's arms—the man who first crossed
      the polished sill
50 years before her. In this upstairs
hall, he draws a halo spotlight to himself,
so young and square-jawed, her forever-
heart's desire. She remembers still.

And in a farther corner, my gray father
circa 1989 laughs as I never knew him
into Esther's marcelled hair.
Buck-tooth smiling, she gives a saucy
fillip with one pump; her skirt
is just the rage for 1927.

A pity Esther had to go home early
from that earthly ball; nor could Heber stay—
leaving my parents
to take each other's hand in a wordless
foxtrot, measuring out the downstairs dance-
floor all those years.

Look, how very happy each one looks
now, dancing in these pairs.

Sky-Blue Tiles

Imagine living in the body
of that lady with the languorous wrist,
and fingers too lax
to hold a rake or lever the handle
of a pump to draw deep water
to a pail.

In this slick magazine photo, everything
flows of itself upward. Fountains
like music of marbled water,
a foreign language where words
themselves are lyrical,
even when spoken by a sullenly handsome
youth who may simply be telling
his girl, "Give me a break."

For such a lady sitting forever
languid, fixed on film
in the fragrance of olives, or wisteria,
the words are of no account.
She breathes an air too fragile
for the dull security
of an everyday Tuesday.

Does that lady know, the aging man
at the next table might be
Merlin, about to transform everything
into magnolias?

Wed by the Justice of the Peace

who just enjoyed a pretty good
supper, by the looks of it—plates
smeared with gravy on the stained white
cloth, and drumsticks gnawed to the bone.

As if they hadn't called ahead, as if
they caught the Justice by surprise
with his vest unbuttoned, eying
the Pope's nose across the platter;
his missus wiping a child's crumbed face
before she clears the table.

And does it matter, for a bride
whose hemline's longer than the fashion,
gray frock worn thin at the collar,
her bouquet a bunch of roadside chicory?

Let her recite her vows before the altar
of pushed-back chairs and crumpled
napkins. For witnesses, stuffed bellies
already hungering for tomorrow's
breakfast biscuits, and these ever-
lasting dishes. Dirty dishes. Let her
learn right now what marriage is about.

for Muriel

My Father's Love Letters

didn't mention his first wife,
and skirted his ten-year-old daughter.

My father's letters to my mother
didn't call on the wind and the sea to witness.
Some weekends, he'd stand beside her
at the cliff-edge, silent.

My father's letters were written
in a hand much too careful, you'd think,
for a physician; tiny, frugal.

My father's love letters to my mother
didn't promise "till death
do us part." They both knew
all about that already.

Fire in the Fingers

for Frank Burritt

$5 a month for treatments for catarrh
through this long satiric winter in St. Paul,
1895. The Smith & Barnes upright piano
rents for $3 a month, music being cheaper
than health. She's a slattern mistress

who keeps you tuning other people's pianos,
your fingers growing stiff and calloused
from the friction of the wires;
giving lessons to strangers' daughters,
whose hands jerk and stutter over the keys
in the best of weather.

Musicians starve without a trade,
but you burn to go to Boston
where the climate is no better, to study more
piano despite the cold
that stings the tips of your fingers,
this everlasting winter.

Back home, your dutiful cousins marry
and milk the dairy cows. Your mother
wonders what odd music plucks the strings
between your heart and head, to drive
a son so far away.

Under the Big Trees

Sequoia National Park 1946

I don't know
the look on this man's face, my father
who almost never smiled.
Who workadays wore gabardine
and got back home too late
for gardening, for tending fruit trees
in the side yard, roses by the door.
This vacation day
in workman's pants tucked
into knee-boots, and a logger's
flannel plaid rolled up
past the elbow, he smiles
and touches fingertip to fingertip
chest-level. He's taller
than I knew him, as if raised
at the shoulders by the tree
that stands behind.
The snapshot lops the tree off
to its massive base: grandfather
of trees.

Mom unexpectedly in jeans
looks out of place, but holds me
steady in this woods-scape
like the fairytales she always
made a little menacing.

It's a dark woods
around this shaft of light
that finds my father
smiling. My father
who truly loved trees.

Vandals

My mother's driving us
through November gray
past miles of leafless vineyards,
gnarled old men in rows.
She's driving to the school
where she keeps a neat cubicle
with eye-charts and thermometers
and sterile gauze.
I'm four. The safe white rooms
of my mother's school this morning
are awash in sticky red
paint flung and smeared against
the walls. A hooligan,
memory x'es out connectors.
In hospital, the nurse
my mother arrives too late
to staunch the blood of the man
whose face is vandalized
by cancer. Dreamlike, memory
goes backwards, then repeats.
I saw none of it. I saw it all.
"Vandalism" is a word too big
for me. I sit in a corner
till I can learn to spell it.

Celebrations

The focus here is a birthday party
in black and white, five little girls
in sun-dresses, sitting on a lawn
before a trellis. Their dresses
are pastel, floral, flounced.
These children haven't had a chance
to develop smudged cheeks or bloody
knees. They just arrived, and someone
told them to look off in the distance
to their left—the way one tosses a pebble
to get a pet dog's best profile.
Someone forgot to say "cheese."
Under parti-colored paper hats
is not a smile. They squint
in three-year-old negative
against the sun. It's somebody's
birthday and they ought to be glad,
there's favors and cake and
not just the birthday-girl's
getting older.

Lost in Two Cars

Somewhere in Nevada my mother
stands on the highway shoulder
beside the old Dodge, waiting
for her second husband, my father
driving the '50 Ford, to miss
her in the rearview mirror.

That's the thing about traveling
in pairs. Even though my father
            turned around at last
with enough daylight left
to fix the flat, and then,
late as it was, find a motel
with a vacancy and a double bed,
and a cot for the child—even then,

it wasn't the way she intended
the trip to turn out.

Longshoreman

All day you've been helping the old man
with his puzzle. It's spread out
on the dining room table like an evening
meal. His latest jigsaw job in 2000
interlocking pieces: outline of a seascape
with lighthouse, a cardboard shoreline
without tides. Missing pieces lie around
the edges, grouped by color, shape or
whimsy wherever they landed,
like bomb debris. He no longer remembers
D-Day, a big bang that shaped the world
as he knew it. Mini-stroke must be
what's left him so far from any shore.
He has a dozen more puzzles
in unopened boxes, in the spare bedroom.
Any occupation, you say, is a blessing.
He used to have a perfect jigsaw mind,
fitting the cargo of a steamer to the last
packet of gaskets and screws
timed right down to the tide.

A Pair of Photographs, 1939

It was just the two of them, of course,
no one else to prove they stood together
this May afternoon on the side of a road

that winds the easy way
over the summit. Widower and widow,
two faces surely meant to gaze together

from a single frame. But here,
beside a wood-paneled station wagon
they strike separate windblown smiles.

For him, she clasps her hands
behind her back and lowers her eyes
against the western sun.

Then she snaps him with one
hand gripping the road-sign like a trophy:
ELEVATION 3000 FT.

Is this how high
love lifted them, the second
time around?

The Heroine Had She Lived

Her lover's been transformed by years.
He's dark-skinned now, and wears
green scrubs. She can't remember where
she left the other, the one she swore

she'd die to marry, as the third act
turned sour. This one lifts her
with a lover's voice more than brute
force, so she sits upright in the chair

and takes her gruel, this bland fare
blended beige like decades. And that other,
blended no doubt into soil and air,
she can't remember. Was it somewhere

before the final scene, she put memory
away, as not being worth the grief?

Contrails

She's dreamed
the steep approaches,
figured the luck
of tail numbers, praying
on the wind. Still
she wishes to be fixed
to her shadow.
      "Up there,
that's where you get a life,"
he tells her, skin
burned at the wrist, his eyes
too bright with sun.
      She loves
the pilot in him, knows
he's lost. She'll cry
the day he flies off
to the next new place.
She'll pick a musky rose
and count the small
planes spiralling through sky.
She'll watch as each
one falls
below horizon, slips
into cloud.

In Sympathy

You posted your loss to the list,
such sad news, and everyone
who knows you or knew your late
departed sends condolences, every-

one on this e-list by REPLY-ALL
goes on sending and receiving
everyone else's sympathy, it seems

everyone's husband has died
in a cyber-overflow of answering
grief, in lines that turn
and return in a ritual like rhyme,

like half-lives, as if it were
our place, each of us, to mourn
all husbands, in reiteration or

anticipation. How many times
shall one's own half die?

The Stranger

This is the face Aunt Ethel brought home
in 1917, perhaps the best man
she ever managed. In oil on canvas
he squints against the sun.

He could be sizing things up:
a blood-bay mare or a trade in sheep,
the breeze off Tunis; what on earth
this foreign lady wants of him.

I never knew this grand-aunt who,
they say, had a talent for the portrait-
likeness. She achieves his homespun
tunic and the red-striped cloth

wound into a turban. But his smile
costs more than American coins can hire.
He turns to her his profile. Observing
askant as she carefully applies pigment,

he grants her the pinched-tight lips,
unblinking scrutiny of worlds
from the corner of the eye
whose gaze she hopes to capture.

How many brush-strokes to convey
a question? His vision has tracked me
as I move across six decades of rooms.
Alive beyond human years,

he hangs now by the east window.
An eye preserved in oils
can watch forever.
But it never has to smile.

Sleeping Alone

You sleep in a solitary bed,
everyone else is gone. This is the darkest,
soundless corner of the house.

You sleep alone, dreaming of a grandmother
you hardly knew
before her mind left home.

You dream her toothless, gaping wordless
as a fish. In dream, a husband
becomes a father, and a father's son.

You sleep alone now, snug inside the walls.
But tonight beside the pillow, your hand
meets something even softer

than family comfort. A small dead bat,
its fine fur silky. It doesn't belong
here, but outside

under stars, where its living kin sail
the dark; warm-bodied as mothers
with their winged children.

Petri Dish

A cultured ancestor has left
the dream-refinements of her breed:
some dregs of perfume in a blue Delft
bottle now, alas, in smithereens.

A grandchild, remanded to you again
in his obscurantist teenies—too old for hugs
and yet not winsome—has plugged
into the hard-drive XP. How could he

erase all your pictures, those fleet
happy moments before anyone was born?
Something's growing in the seams.
A cumulonimbus darkens to a storm.

Just call it Cloud Nine. Then flee
to the deep *ventanas* of the trees.

Run Rebecca Run

Maiden Claiming Race, Hollywood Park

She sits, head lolled back
in her recliner,
not quite asleep again

as claimers gallop off the screen,
the chestnut blinkered
so as not to see

what's coming up behind,

black filly like a flying dream
of childhood,
long black mane

so black it turned a shadow
as the years turned, ticking off
seconds on a stopwatch

to the finish line.
If wishes were
horses.

Things To Do with a Person with Alzheimer's

Clip Coupons
and wonder if she'll squirrel them away
inside the family Bible.

Sort Clothes By Shape And Color
What was her favorite color?

Have Afternoon Tea
and worry she'll hurl the pot
through the window,
just because.

Straighten The Sweater Drawer
and find a missing pair of eyeglasses
hidden inside a cardigan.

Cook Hot Dogs Outside. She loved
to cook, you might say
she set the kitchen on fire.

Make A Family Tree Poster
where all the women
Finish Famous Sayings and

Feed The Ducks,
Make Paper Butterflies, and

Look Up Names In The Phone Book,
none of the names
their own.

An Only Daughter

In 1947 you were an ancient child
staring from the shadow of your eyes.
You aged a generation in these years,
surviving link of elder lines.

Staring from the shadow of your eyes
a first grader confronts the lens,
surviving link of elder lines
meant to keep your family going.

A first grader confronts the lens
and then skips down the hall.
Meant to keep your family going,
you pose as freshman, Xmas '59.

And then skips down the hall
everything you cram into your brain.
You pose as freshman, Xmas '59,
under a weight of texts, so heavy

everything you cram into your brain
settles in your hooded smile
under a weight of texts. So heavy—
as the world through parents' eyes

settles in your hooded smile—
by 1960 you were as ancient, child,
as a world through parents' eyes.
You'd aged a generation. Years.

The Diner

She's holding us up again. In her post-life
she's given up on responsibility.
It's starting to snow, you're idling the pickup
in the parking lot, you say we need
to get home. I dart through the grocery aisles.
She isn't there. In the diner next door
she sits primped at the formica counter,
looking as she did in her 50s, her face
used up but not yet famished. The waitress
sets down a plate of sad meatloaf under gravy
while she goes on talking to a perfect stranger.
This must be her formerly childless life
when she was happy. I tell her we have
to leave, it's snowing. She keeps on talking,
gesturing. She's wearing a tall
black feather head-dress and dark furs.
Is this the cape from her first marriage,
the two dead fox-heads with paws
draped across the throat? The one
she left me like her prize possession?
It's still hanging in my closet
under a sheet, shedding hairs. I can't
get rid of it, horrible red ghost grinning.
Her voice grows louder as if she were drunk
on this raw day in a diner that serves nothing
but coffee. I pick her up and carry her
out the door like a pet dog. How light she is,
no larger than a small monkey.
Like a monkey, warm, fuzzy and a little
damp. It's snowing.
You and the pickup are gone.

Jacaranda

We agree on this,
it's never been so gray.
The sky won't rain.
The concrete entrance drive,
the stucco portico.
In the wings, old people

kept from dying.
We've got a hundred papers
to sign. We're at a loss
for florid verse. And yet,
when no one's listening,
we beg each other

for a word. Out the window
a jacaranda—exotic tree
with extravagant
cerulean blooms in summer—
droops its winter-
feathered leaves.

Imagine her in blue
boas, flamenco on a breeze.
Imagine
so we can't forget.
At the tip of every twig
a castanet.

Walking Your Dreams

Other people wear out their shoes,
walk holes in the heels of their socks.
Your feet fidget through the nights,
sandpaper soles against the sheets.

I bought this floral fitted pair
not five months ago; already a rip
foot-level, the weave worn through.
You won't sleep still; you wander.

In the morning you can't describe
the dreams that keep you moving.
I'll buy new sheets at Kmart. Soft
gray plaid, unimaginative and cheap.

Eighty-eight and Counting

The old man stares ahead, no reason why.
The cat's stretched sunning on the kitchen sill,
and now a flight of crows across the sky.

He's got a jigsaw puzzle lying by
half-finished years ago, a test of skill.
The old man stares ahead. No reason why

he couldn't turn the pieces where they lie;
but fitting things together calls for will.
And now a flight of crows across the sky

casts shadows. Do they mean to clarify
some age-old question about good and ill?
The old man stares ahead. No reason why.

For supper, Elena's fixing chicken pie.
She always sees an old man gets his fill.
And now a flight of crows across the sky.

If asked, he whispers he would rather die.
But she just wipes her hands. With time to kill,
the old man stares ahead, no reason why,
and now a flight of crows across the sky.

Housekeepers

Every morning is a surprise:
here's a brittle bouquet
in lemon-yellow and lettuce-green
on the kitchen sink, with a single
spiked orange blossom set off-center
in a plain blue vase.

Who could have left it there?
How long ago since she arranged
flowers? For years now,
you don't sleep well, you miss her
floating from bedroom curtain to hall,
reorganizing things. By morning
everything's different

except her faded perfume on the air.
You check her vanity again,
she isn't there. Paid ladies
keep the house. This must be their
new game of hide and seek,

that leaves a chill
of what isn't anymore,
and smudges a lost finger-
print
across the pane of dawn.

Tonight at The Yellow Rose

Out on the floor
a blue jeans wrangler dances
with his partner in pastel, an easy
Texas two-step as the leather
boot-soles glide, skirts swirl,
the patterns change.
The lights are dim enough,
you don't see faces, only feel
the pulse of fingers,
swing-steps steady
to the beat.

Country love-songs catch
like fishhooks in the throat
you can't pull back, not even
when you're in love with someone
who isn't anymore—no matter
how he loved to dance.
                Tonight
it doesn't matter
who's your partner. Skirts
swing and heels click, the music
is the same old songs of wanting.

Tonight you'll be dancing
with your cowboy.

90th Birthday

Balloons in bunches
and the table's heaped with goodies
he can't eat.
He's propped in a hospital chair
that assumes all positions except
release. The oxygen cannister
stands guard.
We sit around the edges
in whispers. The Pope has died.
But someone's brought a camera
so we group around
the sheeted man. Great-grandkids
and aging friends; the woman
who used to cook his meals.
We smile for the flash.

When the film's developed
there's this shot, grainy and dark
as a Rembrandt:
the old cook bends to the marble
skull, her cheap print dress
against his hospital gown.
Madonna and ancient child.
Eternal lovers clasping
veined hands.
She kisses his bare scalp
or maybe she whispers something
none of us can understand.

A Woven Line

> *Old sea-captain rests in neat little cottage by the sea.*
> —Sabian symbol for 13 degrees Leo

He wakes from dreams of knots, or nets,
a sort of word-play in which lines entwine
into a sling for catching unstrung rhymes.
The rocking sing-song teases him from sleep.

And so he lies here on the dark-side of dawn,
under a great dry ocean of stars—those bright
over-hands across the intervals of night.
Beyond his window, a sweep and chirp
of surf that sounds like all the sea's bats
coming home to roost in shingle, settling
their tidal wings to sleep until the next
incarnation of the moon.

        He doesn't go to sea
except in dreams. Today, he'll gather
what it brings: shells and fishing floats
in bubbled glass and cork, wave-rubbed spars
and sculpted driftwood, everything remade
by salt and sand. Each form individual
with all its details gone. He'll sort and mend,

his way of knotting time into the net laid
over sky and sea. The space between
the netted twine is for breathing out
and into, for letting thoughts billow
into waves. For working arthritic fingers
into bowlines, over-hands and the fixed
square-knot. For stars in their intricate
infinite figure-8s of time.

Death the Linguist

I'm feeling light-headed dreamy
when he calls me
Querida, so I hardly wonder
how he can do that "d" that sounds
like "th" not quite touching
behind the teeth
when he hasn't even got a tongue.
Breeze as soft as blue breath
fading into whisper, a sigh
that rises from below the sternum,
what might be the solar plexus
if he had an ounce of flesh.
He speaks of *Sehnsucht* for a land
I've never visited and always
wished to go, or perhaps
some place I once was and somehow
got broken off from,
a place where all languages
are fluent and all genders agree.
And now he's stringing sounds
I'm almost gone enough
to understand. Maybe they mean
"the hoisin sauce is such
a bargain" in Vietnamese or
"blue tiles of the Lion Gate"
in an ancient Moorish dialect.
It doesn't matter.
I close my eyes and open
my lips to let the tongue
float free.